PEEPERS 2

Peepers 2

Just
Between Us

Pittman Articles & More

Dedications

I dedicate this book to you, the Reader. May this book bring you as much joy as the first. As always, I am humbled and grateful to share my gifts and talents with each of you.
Read, Laugh, & Enjoy,
D. D. Miles

Psalm 8:3-9

Acknowledgments

      First giving all honor and glory to God, I'd like to thank my mother, Janice Williams for her loving support. It's not every day that you have an avid reader, who so happens to be a retired Language Arts teacher, at your disposal. So if my subjects and verbs do not agree, or perhaps you come across some misspelled words, blame her. I'm just kidding, but thank you, mommy, for everything. You are priceless. To my dad, Larry Gosha who is my cheerleader and very supportive. I thank you, dad, for everything as well; your encouragement matters greatly. Thank you to my family and friends for your support as well. As you can see, I can't take full credit for any of this. I am so grateful to those who have come into my life to inspire and motivate me. To you, I say thank you as well.

Chapter 1

With excitement in the air for their granddaughter Kenya's up-and-coming wedding, the last thing the Abrams family wanted to deal with was a family emergency. Walter and Birdie had just returned home from picking up his suit from a men's shop on Third Avenue when they saw Alfreda up on a ladder washing her windows.

"Will you look at this crazy woman? She shouldn't be up there on that ladder." Walter said.

"Well, it's not like she had a choice. She asked her son, but he was too busy. **Oh my God, Walt, Alfreda!**" Birdie said as she saw Alfreda fall. "**Alfreda,** Alfreda, are you okay?"

Birdie asked, leaning over her friend. "Let me help you up." She said, reaching for her. "I think I need an ambulance. I can't move," Alfreda said in agonizing pain. She remembered the conversation between her and her son, J.J. She had called him about her windows weeks ago, but being a police detective kept him busy. Unfortunately for her, windows were not his number one priority. The crime was, and it was at an all-time high in the city. He explained to her why he couldn't take off and made an offer to hire someone to do it for her, but that was not good enough. She told him she felt uncomfortable having strange people around her house and that she would do it herself before hanging the phone up. Now she laid there full of regret and pain.

"Walt! Call nine-one-" She didn't get the other one out, because Fire and Rescue were barreling down their street. "Don't worry, honey," she told Alfreda. "Everything is going to be okay. Now that the Medics are here, I'm going to grab your purse and lock your door. We'll be right behind you." She told her, trying to put on a brave face.

Walter and Birdie followed the ambulance to the hospital. "I have to call her son. Maybe now he'll come to see about his mother. I ought to give him a piece of my mind. She shouldn't have been up there on that ladder, anyway."

"Birdie, stay out of those folks' business now. You know his job is demanding." "It ain't that doggone demanding. Hello JJ, this is Ms. Birdie. Yeah, son, I'm fine. He's fine too. Listen, I'm calling to tell you, there was an accident and your mother fell off a ladder. She is being taken to the hospital. Princeton, I believe. And son, please don't take your precious time by getting there either." She told him before hanging up.

"**Birdie!**" Walter shouted.

"**What!** I guarantee you, she was up there because of him."

"You don't know that."

"Humph, grits ain't groceries if I don't."

Chapter 2

Everyone was waiting in the lobby in hopes of some good news. Birdie had never seen her friend in such a way and didn't know what she would do without her. So she continued to pray and ask God for a full recovery on Alfreda's behalf.

"Johnson family," the woman called out.

"Yes, I'm here. I'm her son, Joe Johnson. Is my mother going to be all right? Can I see her?" He asked anxiously.

"Sure, Mr. Johnson. Follow me. I'm Dr. Carraway of orthopedics and they have assigned your mother to me." That was all Birdie could hear as they walked down the hall. It took everything in her to stay seated. Alfreda is like a sister to her, and she needed to know what was happening. Although she didn't want to, she knew she had to stay in her place and wait. But waiting was not her strong suit.

"I wonder what's taking him so long to come back." She said to Walter.

"He's getting information and spending time with his mother, Birdie. He'll be back soon." Walter replied.

"This is just too much for me. I can't take it. I need to get me some answers. All this waiting is making my nerves bad." She said, shifting from side to side.

"You'll do no such thing, Birdie Abrams. Your impatience is causing your nerves to be bad, nothing else."

"Listen, that's my friend back there, and if I want answers, I'm going to get them." She said while standing.

"Okay, hotshot. Lets see you try to get some, then." Walter said, grinning at her.

"Think I won't? You just watch and see." Birdie said, before storming off.

"Some people don't believe a black cow can give white milk on a Tuesday, but you're about to learn today." He told her as she brushed past him.

And as quickly as she left, she returned.

"Well?" Walter asked, already knowing the hospital's policy.

"Walter Abrams, don't say nothing to me. They wouldn't tell me a doggone thing!

Talking about if I wasn't family bullcrap, they couldn't give out any information. They didn't think that when they asked me for her insurance card and billing information. Besides, I'm just as close to her as her birth sister. What a stupid policy to have?"

"You, of all people, would think that. They have to protect the privacy and the rights of their patients. This is so that ole Joe Blow or nosey Birdie can't just walk off the street and ask what's wrong with people." Walter explained.

"All I'm saying, Walter is - "

JJ interrupted her, "Ms. Birdie, my mother is asking for you,"

"Thank God! Come on, Walter! Where is she!?" She rushed down that hallway as fast as her little feet would carry her. She had never been so excited to see anyone in all her life. "Alfreda, you scared the daylights out of me, girl." She said, giving her a gentle hug. "Birdie, I'll be fine. I just have to stay here while they finish running some tests. I'll be home in no time."

"Thank you, Jesus! Is there anything I can do or get for you?" Birdie asked her.

"No, Birdie, I'm okay for now." She said.

"Okay, well, Walter called the church to place you on the prayer list, and the Deacons will be here visiting other church members in the hospital tomorrow, so I'll come with Walter and visit with you then."

"Yeah, Alfreda, get your rest, and I'll bring Birdie back tomorrow." "Thanks, Walter. I'll see you all tomor-." She said, dosing off.

"Wow, whatever they gave her, I need to put some in my purse to go." Birdie said.

"Ms. Birdie, you are a trip." JJ said, laughing.

"Chile, anything that can make you fall asleep like that, we all need. We don't want any of that Michael Jackson kind of medicine. That didn't turn out so well. I want a good night's sleep without having to rest in peace to get it."

"Now you see why I don't take her places." Walter said, laughing.

"We'll be seeing y'all tomorrow before they have a new patient with a concussion." She said, rolling her eyes at Walter.

"Officer, you heard her threaten me, do your duty, arrest her or something, just violent for no reason."

All JJ could do was raise his hands up and laugh. He was not about to get on Ms. Birdie's bad side no more than he already was.

Chapter 3

After Birdie and Walter left the hospital yesterday, Alfreda's son called to give her his mom's new room and phone number. She couldn't wait to see her friend today. She was going to bring her a few snacks and the latest pieces of gossip.

"Alfreda! How are you feeling?" Birdie asked, concerned.

"I'm very sore."

Before Birdie could ask her anything else, the doctor and Alfreda's son walked into the room.

"Good afternoon Ms. Johnson, I'm Dr. Carraway. I saw you yesterday when they brought you into the E. R. Can you tell me why a seventy-." Alfreda, clearing her throat, caused the doctor to pause. Everyone knew what that meant. Don't tell her age, and the good doctor didn't.

Well, can you explain to me what you were doing up on that ladder at your age?"

"Because I needed my outside windows cleaned, and I got tired of hearing I'll do it Saturday."

"Well, momma, you know I work a lot and would do it. You didn't have to do it yourself.

I even offered to have someone do it for you." Her son said candidly.

"Humph, if I waited on you, I'd never get anything done. I've been telling you for weeks about it. Plus, I also told you that I didn't want any strangers in my house." She told him.

"Well, Ms. Johnson, because you took matters into your own hands, you have a nasty bruise on your left hip. Be thankful because a woman at your age falling could have been worse."

"I understand, doctor, and I'll be more careful in the future. When can I go home?"

"In the future, another nasty fall like this one, and you may not be so fortunate. You won't be going home anytime soon. That bruise requires attention and rehabilitation. So, let's just say you'll be in rehab for the next few weeks."

"A few weeks!" Birdie and Alfreda shouted at the same time.

"Doctor, that's too long," Alfreda pleaded. "I have a wedding to go to, and --"

"And you'll just have to miss it, momma. Your health comes first. I'm sure Kenya would

understand."

"That's a shame, Freda." Birdie told her, trying to console her. But if looks could kill, J.J. would be dead.

"And you know I just ordered my dress, too." She said, disappointed.

"You mean that grey one you showed me, with the sheer sleeves? Oooh, Freda, you would be sharp, honey, with that new hat to match. All you needed was a little handbag, and - -."

"Ms. Birdie!"

"What do you want, and why are you calling my name like that?" Birdie answered. "Because you're not helping matters," he told Birdie. "Look, mom, I know you had your heart set on going, but we only want the best for you. And right now, that's getting well." "You're right, son. I'll do as the doctor has said." She agreed.

"That's good Ms. Johnson. I will have them set up your admission for later today. Prayerfully, you'll heal quickly and be back home in no time." The doctor told her before leaving.

Disappointed, all Alfreda could do was shake her head, acknowledging what the doctor had just told her. She was just getting ready to sulk when she heard a knock at the door.

"Come in," JJ said. "Looks like you have more company coming in, mom." "Who's that, Birdie?" Alfreda asked curiously.

"Oh, that's the Hospitality Ministry. The Deacons are here to visit and pray with you." Birdie replied.

"Oh, my goodness! Tell them to hold on for a second. Let me get dressed." Alfreda said, trying to straighten up in the bed.

"Get dressed? Honey, you're in the hospital, in a hospital gown. Why do you need clothes?" Birdie asked her.

"I don't. But I can put my teeth in and my wig back on. Now hush up and hand me my hair."

"Lawd, have mercy." Birdie said, rolling her eyes.

"Lawd have mercy, nothing. Girl, hurry up before they see me." Alfreda said, rushing

Birdie. "Okay, now how do I look?" She asked, wishing she had a little face powder and lipstick. "Outside of your wig being crooked, you look fine. I don't see why you're going through all this trouble . . . Hey, y'all. How's everybody doing?" Birdie asked after being stopped in midsentence.

"We're doing well, Sister Birdie. We just stopped by to visit with Sister Alfreda. Your husband and brother will be in shortly. We saved the best for last." Deacon Larry told them.

"Oh, I appreciate you all for coming by," Alfreda said, blushing.

"Mmm-hmm, she sure does." Birdie said as she watched how Alfreda and Deacon Larry were smiling at each other. She had some questions to ask. The last Birdie heard, Deacon Larry was seeing Margaret Ann Mitchell and wondered what was going on with them. Better yet, she'll do better by asking her brother because Walter definitely wasn't going to tell her anything juicy.

"Well, Sister Alfreda, how long did they say you would be here?" Another Deacon asked. "They said I will leave today, but it won't be for home. It'll be for a rehab facility because of my injury."

"I hope it won't be for too long." Deacon Larry said, concerned.

"I bet you don't." Birdie said under her breath. As she watched him give a little squeeze to Alfreda's hand. "Un-huh, this helfa has been holding out on me." She thought to herself, smiling.

Alfreda noticed the wide grin on Birdie's face and asked the Deacons if they had seen many people that day. She was trying to get the heat off of her, but she knew Birdie all too well, and there would be some questions to answer sure enough.

Chapter 4

After Walter and George came in, they prayed for Alfreda and were well on their way, everyone except for Deacon Larry. He wanted to sit with her for a while. Birdie also remained just to see why. But before she could get comfortable, Walter drugged her out of the room.

"So, are you going to tell me what's going on, Judas?"

"Birdie, what are you talking about?"

"Oh, I see. We're going to play crazy today?"

Laughing at her, "Birdie, I'm serious. I don't know what you're talking about."

"So you mean to tell me that you didn't see what I saw?"

"Darling, what did you see?"

"You know doggone well what I saw! I saw Deacon Larry grinning like a chess cat at Alfreda."

"So. What's wrong with that?"

"Nothing, but there's something going on. I can feel it."

He looked over at her and rolled his eyes. "Nothing is going on that you should be concerned about."

"Really. So it's nothing strange about the Deacons staying with people longer than necessary?"

"No, it's not, and if you weren't so nosey, you'd see that too."

"Un-huh. We will see."

"Mind your own business, Birdie. You remember what happened the last time that you didn't?"

"If you bring that crap up one more time, I know something."

"I know you need to mind your own business."

"I will after I finish asking Alfreda all about hers."

***

13

"Hey Birdie, I'm calling to give you my number at this facility. Girl, they got me wired all up. And every little movement is painful. Girl, I don't know about this. They need to let me go home and leave me be." Alfreda told her.

"Well, it doesn't look like you'll be there all by yourself. Your new man can come by and help you out."

"What new man?" Alfreda asked her.

"You know, doggone well who I'm talking about, Deacon Larry."

"Birdie, if you don't get off my phone talking crazy. There's nothing going on between me and Deacon Larry."

"That's what your lips say, but I feel it in my bones."

"I don't know what you're over there feeling, but nothing is going on over here. Besides, isn't Larry seeing ah what's her name, Mary, Martha?"

"Margaret."

"Yeah, that's it, Margaret Ann Mitchell. She's a nice lady, too."

"That's what I thought too until I saw the two of you making eyes at each other." "Did you take any of my pain medication while I wasn't looking? Ain't nobody making eyes at each other."

"I know what I saw. And I ain't crazy. Something is going on, and I know it."

"Lady, something is wrong with you," Alfreda said, laughing.

"Un-huh, so you say."

"Let me get off this phone. My pain medicine is finally kicking in. Tomorrow, they are going to start my physical therapy. Please pray they don't kill me. I can barely put weight on that leg."

"I will, and please be careful. Don't let them have you coming out of there walking funny."

"Trust me, I won't," Alfreda said.

Chapter 5

"It's a darn shame. Alfreda had to almost break a hip before her son sent somebody to come by and see about her house." Birdie told her husband as she watched the man out of the kitchen window clean the gutters, then windows.

"Nobody told her to do that. She's just too impatient like most women are." He said, reading his newspaper over breakfast.

"Well, if he had done it the first time she asked him, she wouldn't have been up there in the first place. It's not like she has a man or anything to handle things like that for her, or does she?" She asked, hoping to catch a hint that Walter knew otherwise.

"Whatever you say, Birdie." He said, smiling as he put his plate in the sink." "What's that big smile all about Walter Abrams?" I got him, she thought.

"What, I can't smile at my beautiful wife?"

"You ain't been smiling like that. Looks like you know something that I don't."

Laughing, he replied, "I don't know what you're talking about, woman. Keep it up, and

I'm making you an appointment to go and sit on somebody's sofa."

"Whatever, Walter Abrams. I know what I know."

"Why are you going to blame JJ?" Walter said, changing the subject. "Alfreda knew what needed to be done to that house. How come she didn't call someone herself? Plus, she also knows her son's schedule is very demanding. This was not his fault."

"Well, he's never too busy to be in her kitchen eating up everything day and night. Why not do what she asked? He's there more than he is at home. I know his wife doesn't like that." "You're worried about the wrong things," Walter told her.

"He knows way more people than she does, plus you can't get quotes from any old body.

Nowadays, we can't afford to be that trusting. You hear stories all the time about how senior citizens get reaped off."

"She could ask around too, you know. It's not that hard. People would be more than happy to help her."

"Well, she would be leaving with us tomorrow if he had done what his mother asked him to do."

"Oh, I see the problem now. It's not JJ at all. You're mad because Alfreda is not coming to the wedding."

"Kenya is going to be so disappointed."

"Kenya will be glad just to know if we're there. You really think she's going to be looking around to see who came and who didn't?"

"I still say she's going to be disappointed. I know Alfreda is, and she bought that pretty dress, too."

"That is a shame, but at least she'll have something new to wear to Pastor's Appreciation Day," Walter said, adding insult to injury.

"Ain't nobody thinking about that or you."

Chapter 6

"Walter, I can't believe they made us pay for that extra suitcase." Birdie complained. "I told you not to bring it. You always pack extra stuff that you don't need." Walter told her.

"Well, you never know what's going to happen, and what we might need when we get there. If I left it up to you, we'd only have one suitcase."

"That's because all you need is one suitcase. We're only going to be there for a few days.

When they see our luggage, they wonder if we're moving in."

"Like I said, you never know what we might need. Just like those unnecessary snacks in my carry-on. You know the snacks that you love so much. I'm going to place them right here in the seat next to us." Birdie said.

"You can't do that. That may be somebody's seat."

"Yes, I know. It was Alfreda's. After she got hurt, she canceled her ticket."

"Well, why is the flight attendant pointing someone to this seat?"

"I don't know. After Alfreda canceled, they sold her seat, I guess. Shoot, I sure hope they aren't talkative." Birdie said.

"Excuse me, ma'am, this seat is taken." She said, pointing to the aisle seat. "Can I store your bag in the overhead so that you all will be more comfortable?" Asked the flight attendant.

"No thanks, he will do it later." Birdie told her. "They know they can get on your nerves.

Where is this so-called person?" Birdie asked Walter.

"I'm right here." The woman said.

"Freda!" Birdie screamed as she jumped up to hug her. "What are you doing here?"

"First, let me sit down before I fall down, and I'll tell you." Alfreda said, then taking her seat.

"Oh, honey, I just can't believe you're here."

"You know, I wasn't about to miss Kenya's wedding. I was cutting it close. I didn't think I was going to make this flight."

"Hold on. How are you here? Does your son know where you are?" Walter asked.

"A ride and no. I can't drive just yet."

"Freda, you had a week left. How did you get them to release you so early?" Birdie asked her.

"They didn't, but they can't stop you from getting some fresh air. But no worries, I left them a note."

"A note, oh my God! Our airplane is about to be pulled over because we have a runaway patient." Walter said.

"By the time my son finds out, we'll be halfway there."

"Are you okay to do this, Alfreda?" Birdie asked her with concern.

"Girl yeah, I'm fine. I'm just slower than I used to be."

"They're going to stop this plane from taking off. I just know it." Walter was telling them.

"They won't if you sit back and be quiet." Birdie told him.

"I'm telling you, Birdie. They will stop this plane." He said.

Over the PA system, they heard, "Attention ladies and gentlemen, we have a slight delay.

Please remain seated."

"Didn't I tell you?" He told them.

"That could be for anything." Birdie replied.

"Well, why are they reopening the doors? That's not sup- posed to happen. Here we go."

"Excuse me, Ms. Johnson," the flight attendant said to Alfreda. "I apologize, but we almost left your walker. I had it stored for you." She said apologetically.

"Oh, thank you baby so much," Alfreda told her. "Whew," Alfreda said after the flight attendant left.

"Alfreda honey, whew chile. I thought they had caught up with you." Birdie said, laughing and relieved.

"Me and you both, I was holding my breath for dear life," Alfreda told her.

"Honey, Walter is sitting over here overreacting like you are a fugitive running from the law with a suitcase full of drugs and money."

Walter, on the other hand, didn't find any of it funny. The next voice they heard was from the captain saying that they were clear for takeoff.

Chapter 7

"That wasn't too bad. Was it Birdie?" Alfreda asked as she took off her seatbelt.

"Not at all. I wonder who's meeting us. Walt, who's coming to get us?"

"I think one of those children."

Birdie just looked at him. "Yeah, Walter, but which one?"

"I don't know. I guess we'll find out when we get to the airport." He said, annoyed.

DCA was as busy as ever. After leaving the baggage claim, they started looking for familiar faces. Alfreda was glad she had phoned a few days ahead to let them know she'd be needing their wheelchair service. There was no way she could've walked long distances.

"Hey, isn't that Karen over there?" Walter asked.

"Where?" Birdie asked.

"Standing over there in the yellow dress."

"Yes. That's our baby. Karen!" Birdie yelled to get her attention.

"Mother! Daddy!" She said, hugging them. "Ms. Alfreda! Oh, my goodness. What happened to you?" She asked, not knowing about the accident.

"Hey, Karen! Girl, I just had a little fall. You look so pretty." She said, giving her a gentle hug.

"Thank you, Ms. Alfreda. I'm sorry to hear you've hurt yourself. Daddy, you'll have to help me get her wheelchair in the trunk." "No, I don't. She can walk."

"Daddy, she's in a wheelchair, and -"

"Will you let her know that you can walk, so she won't go into this long-drawn-out explanation of why not?"

"He's right, Karen. I can with the help of my walker, but not long distances."

"Oh, okay. Daddy, you could've just told me that."

"Karen, I am tired and hungry. Can we go already?" Walter demanded.

"I bet you wished you had asked for some more of them peanuts, like Alfreda and I did, huh?"

"Birdie, them peanuts weren't going to do nothing but make me angry. I want some real food. How far are we from the hotel?" He asked Karen.

"Not too far." She answered.

"How come Kenya and Stephen didn't come with you?" Birdie asked.

"Oh, mother, they are busy getting ready for tonight's festivities." "What festivities?" Birdie asked.

"Well, since the wedding isn't for a few days, his family decided to host a Caribbean night for their engagement party. They are preparing all the food, and there will be a live band there too."

"You mean food from his country? Like what?" Birdie asked.

"You know, like crab, chicken, rice, red beans, fried plantains, stuff like that." "That doesn't sound too bad, Birdie," Alfreda told her.

"We'll see. Y'all know I can't be eating all that funny food."

"Ooh, it'll be very nice if they did it Carnival style," Alfreda said.

"Half-naked people walking around in costumes. I don't think they'll allow that at the Four Seasons."

"We are talking about Washington D. C. Ain't no different than any old regular day," Alfreda said. "Speaking of which, will we see any sites along the way?" She asked.

"I know. I'm ready to go. The only sight I want to see is a plate with some food on it." Walter said.

"Well, Ms. Alfreda, I could take you to see the White House."

"I pass. I could have stayed home and watched the news if I wanted to see struggle and disappointment in action. Besides, I saw enough of it when I taught school. Show me something else, honey." She said.

Walter was standing there glaring at them when Birdie noticed the dirty looks he was giving. "Come on y'all. He's like a grizzly bear when he's hungry." Birdie said.

"Yeah and if I don't eat something soon, I'm going to bite one of y'all." He told them. "You just shoulda got the peanuts like we did. You ate your snacks up before we could even leave Birmingham good. Now you wanna boss us around because you are hungry." Birdie said as they fussed through the airport.

Chapter 8

"Girl, this hotel is nice that we're staying in." Alfreda said to Birdie, as she looked around the hotel lobby.

"It sure is. I can't believe that my baby is days away from getting married."

"Yeah, and I especially love that all we have to do is get dressed and come on down." "Freda, that's the best part!" Birdie replied.

"I still say they should've gotten married in a church. What's wrong with a church wedding?" Walter chimed in.

"Oh, you can talk to us with some sense now that we have fed you. There's nothing wrong with where they're getting married, Walter. That's what they wanted to do. Besides, we didn't have a church wedding either, and we're just fine." Birdie told him.

"I beg your pardon, Birdie Abrams, but as my memory serves me right. Yes, we did." He told her.

"I beg your pardon, Walter Abrams, but your memory has served you wrong because we got married in the Pastor's study."

"And where is the Pastor's study?"

"At the church."

"Exactly! We had a church wedding."

"Man, that's not the same thing as a church wedding." She said, laughing at her husband.

"It is in my book." He said, proving his point.

"Only you would think a thing like that, Walter."

"Facts are facts, baby. We got married down there at the church house, and they should, too."

"A wedding is a wedding no matter where it happens. It will have no effect on the marriage itself. You're just bothered by the fact that your baby girl is getting married. That's your problem, Walter Abrams."

"I wouldn't say all of that, Birdie, because if it were her and Darius, we'd have to lock you up in a closet somewhere."

"And I thank God for small favors." She said, lifting her hands.

Clearly annoyed and slightly embarrassed, Karen interrupted the latest round of debates. The last one was a no-win. Who made the best hamburgers? Who cares was her thoughts? She loved her parents, but she couldn't wait to get them inside their hotel room, and here they go again. "Can y'all please check-in and stop entertaining the other guests in the lobby?" Karen asked them. "Ms. Alfreda, I don't know what you're going to do with them?" "Me either, but they know they tickle me." She said, laughing.

"Oh no, here comes trouble," Karen said, referring to her Uncle George and her brother Kasey. Those two are like two peas in a pod. When they get together, it's never a dull moment.

"Hey, darling, how's my favorite niece doing?" Her Uncle said, giving her a huge hug.

"Our baby is getting married in a couple of days. I know she'll be as beautiful as you were."

"Thanks, Uncle George, but you call all of your nieces your favorite." She said, laughing.

"Girl, I only mean it when I'm talking to you." He replied jokingly.

"You know what? You're a hot mess."

"Well, it's true." He told her, then realized Alfreda was standing next to her. "Sister Alfreda, is that you? Oh my goodness lady, what are you doing here? They said you'd be rehabbing for a while." He asked, concerned.

"Hey, Deacon George, I wouldn't miss Kenya's wedding for anything in the world. You had to know that I'd be here." She told him.

"Well, it's good seeing you up and about."

"As they say, Deacon, it's better to be seen than viewed any day. So while I have the time and energy, I'm living it up."

"Well, I heard that." He said, laughing.

Kasey and his parents joined his sister, uncle, and Ms. Alfreda.

"Well, look at my favorite couple," George said.

"Let him tell it. We're his favorite, everything," Walter said, kidding.

"Not everything, Walter. I like my other brother-in-law twice as much as I do you. It's his wife that works my nerves." George replied.

"Now, you just wait a minute! You're talking about our sister." "Yes, I know." He said, causing them all to laugh.

George and Walter had gone back and forth like this since the day they met years ago.

George couldn't have found a better friend in Walter and was very proud to call him brother.

"Hey, y'all," Walter said. "Help me prove Birdie wrong. Where were we married?" "At the church, Dad," Kasey answered.

"See, I told you, and he wasn't even there." He said, pointing at Kasey.

"I'm not about to debate this with you. We need to go to our rooms, and you over here asking crazy questions. I think they put something in that burger you ate."

"Don't get huffy with me because my son proved you wrong." He said winking and smiling at Kasey.

"Our son has done nothing of the sort." Birdie replied.

"Mom, dad, Ms. Alfreda, don't forget about Caribbean night. It's in a couple of hours. So get some rest, and we'll see you all soon." Karen said, bringing a close to the great debate by rushing them into the elevator.

Chapter 9

"Hurry up, Walter, Alfreda is waiting for us." She told him after hanging up the phone from Alfreda.

"Being on that walker, she's not in a rush to go anywhere fast."

"Leave her alone. She's doing good to be here. I don't know what I'd do if something worse had happened."

"So you've said. Go ahead and get her, and I'll meet y'all in the hall." He said, looking around to make sure he wasn't leaving anything he needed.

Birdie stepped across the hall to knock on Alfreda's door. "Come in." Alfreda said.

"Girl, you don't be inviting people-"

"Shhh." Alfreda said to Birdie, with her index finger pressed against her lips. "Yeah, baby, grandma loves you too. Un-huh, all right now. You too, have a good night and kiss the boys for me. All right, goodbye." She said, hanging up. "Sorry about that. That was Pepper.

Honey, that girl knows she can talk."

"Always could." Birdie said under her breath.

"She always calls me around this time of night. I appreciate her for checking in on me."

"That's sweet."

"Especially now, since her dad told her about my fall. It took everything to keep her from coming home."

"There's nothing wrong with that. To have people who care about you is always a good thing."

"Yeah, you're right. Are we ready to go eat some of this good Caribbean food?" Alfreda asked her, walking to the door.

"As I ever gon' be, I guess." Birdie replied.

Walter joined them in the hall.

"Hey Walter, looking sharp," Alfreda told him.

"Thank ya, thank ya. I clean up every now and then." He said, grinning.

"Come on y'all. We gotta see what this Caribbean night is all about." Birdie told them.

"I bet it's going to be very nice. Where did Kenya say Stephen was from again, Birdie?" "One of those countries over there in the Caribbean." She replied while moving over to

allow others on the elevator. "I just hope the food is good."

"I'm sure it will be Birdie. Stop worrying." Her husband told her.

"That's easy for you to say. You're coming half-full. Alfreda and I are ready to eat."

When the doors opened to the ballroom, the fragrance of sweet pineapple, coconut, jerk seasoning, and rum welcomed them. The air filled their nostrils with the promise of something delicious. Stephen's family had spared no expense for this event. Their menu consisted of succulent lobster tails, spicy Caribbean, and coconut shrimp. Mouth-watering jerk and curry chicken, curried goat, crab legs, oxtails, and fried plantains. They also had Caribbean flavored sides of rice and beans, corn, coleslaw, salad, and several beautiful fruit arrangements.

If the fragrance of food hadn't swept them away, the sheer and long fabrics in beautiful hues of gold, green, fuchsia, and turquoise that flowed in unison sure did. Every guest glided across the floor in rhythm to the smooth sounds of the Calypso band with a tropical drink in their hand. Tonight was surely going to be a night to remember.

"Oh girl, this is so nice." Alfreda said, looking around the room.

"It sure is, Alfreda." Birdie replied in awe.

"I'm ready to eat, honey. I think I will start with some jerk chicken and shrimp." Alfreda said. That curried goat looks good too."

"I don't know about that. That sounds like it may raise my blood pressure." Birdie said, looking over the food.

"Good evening, everyone." Karen said. "Please take your seats, and I'll have a server fix your plates."

"Sounds good to me, honey. Thank you." Alfreda said.

"Hey, Karen, tell them to give me a little bit of everything," Walter said.

"Mother, would you like the same?" She asked.

"No, chile. This here stuff will run my pressure up. Give me something simple. Where's the menu at?"

"**Mother!** There is no menu. This is it. You mean to tell me with all of this good food that you can't find something here that you'd like to eat?" She asked, trying to mask her frustration.

"I don't. I really don't see anything I would want. But you can tell them to give me some of those wings and rice. Oh, and some of that fruit, I guess that's safe." Birdie said, looking at the caterer's table.

"What about some coconut shrimp, Birdie? They're going to be really good." Alfreda told Birdie, who was now frowning at her. "Hold on and wait one minute. Is that what I think it is? Birdie, look!" Alfreda said, as she pointed at someone's plate passing by.

"**Oxtails!**" They said in unison.

"Now, I didn't see those." Birdie said. I sholl hope they cooked them right."

"Okay, mother, I'll have the plates made and sent to your table." She said relieved.

  ***

Kenya and Stephen made such a beautiful couple. Kenya looked like a bronzed goddess in her long designer fuchsia V-neck formal gown with a high slit. Just like the flowing fabric that decorated the ballroom, with every step she made, her dress flowed with her. Stephen was the perfect complement to her in his tailor-made black suit. They were all smiles as they stood on stage to greet and thank everyone in attendance.

"We would like to thank each of you for joining us to-night. I know many of you have traveled some great distances, whether it was from Trinidad or across the country, to be here with us, we love and appreciate you all dearly. I must say." He said, looking at Kenya, "Since the day this beautiful woman entered my life and finally agreed to be my wife, I didn't think my life could be more amazing. But each day with you, it is. Thank you, my love, for choosing me. I am blessed beyond measure with you in my life and by my side." Stephen said to her before giving her the sweetest kiss.

Stephen's greeting moved everyone. Many clapped, and others cheered. As Kenya prepared to give her greetings, she became overwhelmed with emotion. Stephen held her tightly as she spoke. "Thank you." She said to Trinity, who just handed her a handkerchief. "Umm, what can I say, but thank you?" Gathering her remaining thoughts and wiping away her tears, she said while holding Stephen's hand. "Oh God, I thank you for this man. Please bear with me, family. He just takes my breath away. I am incredibly blessed to have you all here with us, and to be loved and accepted into such a wonderful family." Turning to Stephen, Kenya continued, "Thank you so much, my love, for being everything I prayed for and more. My life has not been the same since you've entered it, and I cannot wait to become your wife." She said before sharing another kiss.

Chapter 10

"Girl, that was so beautiful," Alfreda said, sniffing. "I'm so happy for Kenya." "That's my baby. She sure did us proud." Birdie replied.

"And they make such a beautiful couple. I can't wait to see how she looks in her wedding dress. Have you seen it?"

"Nope, but you know I asked. But her mammy stopped her from showing it to me."

"Why would Karen do that?"

"Because she could. Talking about Kenya should want everyone to be surprised. Or some mess like that. I started to tell her about herself, but Walter was mean-mugging me at the time. And you know, can't nobody say boo to Karen without there being a problem with him."

"Yes, I remember how protective he was about his baby girl, honey."

"Ain't nobody thinking about them. She has always been a daddy's girl. He's the main reason she always had her nose up in the air. And marrying money didn't make matters better. Just because you have two more dollars than the next man, doesn't make you better than anybody else. We are hard-working, humble people, and we raised our children to be the same; to be thankful for everything that we have, but somehow her wires got crossed. She'd always wanted the best of this or the best of that, honey, a mess." Birdie said, throwing her hands up.

"Yep, there's a name for that, Bougie." Alfreda said, looking over at the dessert table.

"Pretty much." Birdie agreed. "Lookout, here comes the queen mother now."

"Mother, Ms. Alfreda, are you all enjoying yourselves?"

"Quite nicely, thank you. Everything is simply beautiful, honey. But I wouldn't expect anything less." Alfreda replied.

"Anything for our little princess. She deserves the very best." Karen said proudly.

Before the conversation could continue, the band had just announced that they were accepting song requests.

"I have a good one too!" Birdie said excitedly. "Come on, Alfreda, we're getting ready to dance now!"

Karen chuckled to herself. She couldn't imagine a song that would bring people to the dance floor, yet alone wanting to hear something that her mother had chosen.

"Hey baby, do y'all know the song Hole in the Wall by Mel Waiters?"

"**Mother!**" she yelled. Then lowered her voice after drawing attention. "This is a Calypso band, not the jukebox at Ray's Blues and Barbeque." She said snidely.

"Well, why ask for a music request, then?"

"They don't play that type of music," Karen told her.

Seeing the tension between the women, the man replied, "Ma'am, we can have the DJ play that song for you and any others that you'd like. DJ hit it!"

Birdie left Karen standing there looking like a wet poodle while she, Alfreda, and Alfreda's walker hit the dance floor, to swing their hips from left to right. Before long, they had company, including the happy couple to be.

"Dear, what's the matter?" Karen's husband asked as he approached her.

"Honey, look at this. My mother has ruined Kenya and Stephen's engagement party."

"No, she hasn't, honey, look. Everyone is having a wonderful time. They're up laughing and dancing, enjoying themselves, even my side of the family, and you know how stuffy they can be. It must be the rum." He said, laughing.

Karen didn't see the humor in any of it. What she saw was a clear disaster. "Honey, just go back to our suite and get some rest until the mother-in-law tea tonight. Did you invite your mother and Ms. Alfreda?"

"Oh Heavens, no! She'd find some way to ruin and embarrass me there, too. Thank goodness she doesn't know about it."

"Go on up, and I'll check on you later. I'll take care of things down here." He said, then kissed her on the cheek.

Karen agreed with her husband and proceeded to leave. But before exiting the ballroom, she saw her husband joining in with the others on the dance floor to Beyonce's version of Before I Let Go.

"**Traitor**," she exclaimed before leaving.

Chapter 11

"Birdie, I haven't danced like that in years. But girl, if we're going to Kenya's bachelorette party tonight, I need a nap." Alfreda told her as they walked to their rooms.

"I hear you, Alfreda. I'm going to get some rest myself and check on Walter. The poor man almost ate himself to death."

"Girl, that was until they played that Jackie Wilson's, Baby Workout. He stopped eating then." Alfreda said, laughing.

"That's how I knew he had eaten too much. Honey, we used to tear that song up back in the day."

"Plus, we are a little older, Birdie. He can't do all those spins and dips like he used to, but y'all still got it, Sister."

"Honey, I thought you were gonna hurt yourself when they played that Sam Cooke's, Having a Party." Birdie said, laughing at the thought.

"Girl, you and I both! That's why I sat down immediately after. I forgot that I was on a walker for a reason. It was that dip that got me into trouble fooling around with that brother of yours."

"That brother of mine loves to dance, honey. George was still on the dance floor dancing with Kenya when we left."

"Lawd, I hope he doesn't wear out the child's poor feet before she has time to dance as husband and wife with her husband."

"Chile, Kenya kicked those heels off a while ago. She knows her great-uncle. Well, girl, I'll knock at your door when I'm ready." Birdie said, entering her room.

"See you later, Birdie," Alfreda told her before entering her own.

***

"Well, well, well, if it isn't the dancing queen."

"What are you talking about, Walter?"

"You had a good time, I see."

"I sure did, and I see you did, too. I just told Freda that I thought you were gonna eat yourself to death."

"Birdie, that food was soooo good. I gave my compliments to the chef. And Stephen's family had prepared all of it. They can invite me to their family reunion, Christmas dinners, or just because if they cook like that all the time." Walter said, laying on the sofa like a fat cat.

"You ate like I haven't fed you in months of Sundays." Birdie said, shaking her head.

"It was just too good."

"I'm surprised you didn't take a to-go plate when you left."

"Who didn't? Yes, I did! Well, my baby had one prepared to be delivered to me before she left."

"She left, why?" That was odd of Karen to leave the party, she thought.

"Yeah, she told me, she had a tea planned with some of the ladies in Stephen's family and a few of her friends. Are you and Alfreda going too?"

"No."

"Why wouldn't you want to attend" You're the grandmother of the bride." He asked, concerned.

"Because Karen didn't invite us, Walter." She said as the words stung.

"What do you mean, you all weren't invited?" He asked, confused.

"It's like I said. She didn't invite us."

"Oh yeah, we're going to get this straight. Now she has done some strange things, but not to invite you, I don't think so." He said, pulling out his phone to call Karen.

"Walter Abrams, put that phone down!"

"Why!"

"Because I don't want to attend a stuffy tea! Especially with all those, bougie women."

"But Birdie, you should be there too."

"I know how you feel, Walt. But I'd rather go to Kenya's bachelorette party tonight."

"Kenya's bachelorette party? Birdie, those young girls won't be comfortable with you and Alfreda there."

"It will be okay. I can give them some good wifely advice."

"I don't like this at all, Birdie, and you know it."

Birdie was shocked. She had never seen her husband upset with their daughter. But little did he know, this was not the first time, nor would it be the last. Karen has had many events that they weren't cordially invited to, but he never knew it, and she didn't have the heart to tell him. He'd be so upset to learn that their daughter didn't think they were good enough to be around her friends. She quickly caught on when she had asked years ago about coming to visit them. Her daughter had declined the offer and insisted that she and her husband would come and visit them, and for years this had been their arrangement. Birdie never asked her daughter why, nor did she have the heart to hear the reason.

Kasey, their son, was totally different. He and his sister were like night and day. If Kasey had it his way, he'd have his parents move in with him and his family in Florida. But they wouldn't dare do that. As a minister, Kasey made his parents very proud. It was an honor to know that he would also be the one to officiate the wedding of Kenya and Stephen.

As Birdie sat there reflecting on the lives of her children, she was blessed and couldn't complain. Her daughter's choices were her own. She loved her despite everything. "I know it,

Walt. But it is okay." She lied. It was hurtful, and now he was aware of how they'd been treated as her parents.

He'd let it go for now, but you better believe Walter Abrams would get to the bottom of things. He didn't appreciate his wife being left out and thought it was very disrespectful. "Okay, baby." He told her. "Well, enjoy yourself tonight."

"I sure will. I'm looking forward to it." Birdie said, smiling at her husband.

***

Birdie only knocked once before Alfreda quickly opened the door. She placed her finger up to her lips to tell Birdie not to say anything.

"Yes, baby, grandma loves you too. Hug the boys tight for grandma. Oh honey, no, you don't have to come. Grandma is doing just fine and will be home before you know it. Come and see me then, okay? All right, grandma gotta go. All right, love you, un-huh, all right. Talk to you soon. Goodnight. Bye now." Alfreda said, hanging up her cellphone. "Girl that Pepper knows she can talk, Jesus! I've been trying to hang up with her for the past 15 minutes."

Laughing, Birdie says, "I wonder where she gets that from?"

"Helfa, I know you're not talking about me."

"And is, and you know it." She said, laughing.

"Come on, and let's go get our party on!" Alfreda said, grabbing her purse.

"We will, but first, let me tell you this. How about Karen is having a tea, and she didn't invite her own mother to it?"

"Say what?" Alfreda said shocked.

"You heard me. That helfa didn't invite me to another gathering, but what makes matters worse is Walter knows about it."

"Oh, no! What did he say?"

"He wanted to confront her, but I told him not to."

"Now you know he is."

"Yeah, but let's hope it's after the wedding."

"So, what are we doing? Are we crashing or what?" Alfreda asked with a devilish grin.

"You're so bad, but nope. We're going to do what we said. She'll have her day."

"Alrighty, lead the way. But you know, I'm good for a crashing. I've had a nap and everything." Alfreda said, following Birdie out of the door on her walker.

"Girl, come on here." Birdie said, laughing at Alfreda.

Chapter 12

The bachelorette party was in full swing. Drinks were flowing, and the music was blasting. It was a wonder that anyone could hear a knock at the door.

"**Surprise!**"

"**Oh my God!** Kenya told me you would not make it!" Trinity shouted.

"Did you think that I was gonna miss Ms. Thang's bachelorette party? Never!"

"She is going to flip out when she sees you," Trinity said. "Here we go." They entered another room where the other guests were. Trinity had someone tap Kenya on the shoulder to look in her direction. In Vanna White fashion, she showcased the surprised guest.

"**Pepper!**" Kenya jumped up and shouted. "I thought you weren't coming until tomorrow," she said, hugging her tightly.

"I had to surprise you, but I'm not the only surprise you have here," Pepper said, smiling.

"Girl, what are you talking about? Are you expecting?" Kenya asked.

"Bite your tongue! But I know who is!"

"Pepper, how? You just got here!" Trinity said.

"**Who?!**" Kenya knew Pepper was holding on to some hot tea.

"Well, while I was checking in, your ex-boo was checking in with his expecting wife." She said, making the motion of a baby bump.

"Girl, shut up. He came! Ken, I didn't know you invited him, considering the stunt he tried to pull." Trinity said.

"Girl, what stunt? What happened?" Pepper asked, intrigued.

The ladies went into another room where they could hear one another better.

"Well, the day before his wedding. He being Darius called me." Kenya said, annoyed at the fact that Trinity brought it up.

"Okay and." Pepper said wanting to know more.

"And he was questioning if he was doing the right thing by getting married." Kenya said, as if it meant nothing.

"Girl, say what! I knew I should've come home." Pepper said.

"He asked me if I was sure that it was Stephen that I really loved and not him, and if so, he would walk away to be with me."

"No freaking way! Before your damn wedding, Bro. Wow! Can we talk about it? I mean, obviously, you turned him down, of course, because you're marrying someone else. But ... me being honest, I always thought him and ole girl had moved a little too quick. Six months, y'all.

Who pops the question six months after meeting some-body?" Pepper asked.

"Darius." Kenya said, laughing.

"I guess when you know or think you know, that's what you do." Trinity added.

"I guess. But from everything I've heard about her from you, she seems to be legit, but still Kenya, six months though." Pepper said.

"Let's be fair. It wasn't as if they got married after six months, but a year after their meeting. I can't wait for you to meet Erica, Pep. She's really cool and down to earth. Anyway,

I basically told Darius the truth. I told him that it was Stephen that I loved. He said he understood and hung up."

"No way!" Pepper said.

"But what Trinity also failed to mention was Darius had been drinking and was pretty much drunk out of his mind. I figured it was his fear talking, nothing else." Kenya said.

"Fear my foot. Tell her what happened during the wedding." Trinity demanded.

Rolling her eyes at Trinity, Kenya told Pepper what happened next. "When it was asked, does anyone know why these two shouldn't be married? Darius looked directly at me, or so I thought. Girl, I didn't move a muscle. I sat there, quiet and still. A few seconds later, he returned his gaze back to his bride-to-be."

"Oh, my God! And you invited him to your wedding? Girl, I don't know if that was a good idea." Pepper said.

"It's not at all what you think. He and I talked later at his reception for a long time. I asked him why he was looking so intense at me, and come to find out, he wasn't looking at me at all. He was looking behind me. An uninvited guest had shown up to his wedding."

"Girl, I know you lying. Who was it? No, let me guess, Moet?" Pepper asked.

"Yep," Kenya confirmed.

"Dang, dang, dang, I missed everything. Well, what happened?" She asked anxiously.

"I don't know. I didn't see her. But I overheard a woman telling our grandmothers about it. She said it was a shame how security snatched Moet out of the church. When I tell y'all, we didn't hear a peep. We didn't hear a peep. It happened just that fast. But I guess Darius knew and had prepared. He also told me the night he called, he was just afraid and needed any reason to bail. But he came to his sober senses, and I'm glad he did. Erica is so sweet and good for him. He admitted that marrying her was the best decision he had ever made." Kenya said to them, smiling. She hid the fact that she was almost tempted to say yes to Darius when she was in Birmingham. But she knew where her heart lied, and it was not with him.

They all jumped when Karla, Kenya's sister, came into the room.

"Helfas, I don't know what y'all in here talking about, and please fill me in later. Not to interrupt, but there's a six-foot-two sexy chocolate man out here asking about the bride to be.

Y'all, he is so fine, and he's dressed like a fireman, too. If you don't get your butts out here, there will be nothing left to devour. He can get it all, and put this fire out over here, baby."

You'd thought somebody had yelled out fire how fast they all bolted through that door. Before Kenya could get her dollars out of her pocket, someone else knocked at the door. She didn't know who was late, but they were not about to make her miss out on the action, so she asked Trinity to get the door for her.

All Trinity could hear were the ladies yell, "**Take it off!**" When Trinity reached the door, she received the shock of a lifetime. "Granny Abrams, Ms. Alfreda, we didn't know you'd be here. Oh, you all must have confused this with the tea. It's –" "Nope, we meant to come here." Birdie said, interrupting her.

"Where's the action at, baby?" Ms. Alfreda asked, looking around.

"Right this way," Trinity said, silently praying everybody was dressed and not in a compromising position.

"**Hey now!** That's what I'm talking about!" Alfreda shouted.

"**Granny!**" Kenya shouted.

"**Grandmother!**" Pepper shouted.

The poor stripper was so embarrassed, that he grabbed two pillows to cover himself.

"What's wrong with y'all? Heeey, now stop dancing, baby? I like that there." Alfreda said to him as she waved her dollar.

"Grandma, I thought you were in the hospital. What are you doing here?" Pepper asked.

"Hospital? She's been here with granny. Will someone please tell me what's going on?" Kenya asked.

"We're here to enjoy the bachelorette party. Hey Birdie, doesn't he look familiar?" Alfreda asked Birdie, diverting from their questions.

"He sure does. Hey young man, by any chance could you be related to the Patterson's in Birmingham, Alabama?"

"He sure does look like them. Same eyes and nose indeed. I'd be shocked if he wasn't."

"No, no ma'am, I don't think so." He said nervously.

Kenya left the room to call her mother.

"Mom, please come and get granny. She and Ms. Alfreda have the stripper answering questions about distant relatives and his family's church home."

Karen couldn't answer her daughter for laughing so hard. "Mom, this is not funny." She said, whispering in the phone.

"Oh yes, it is. She's on a roll today. First the engagement party, now your bachelorette party."

"I thought they would be attending the tea tonight."

"Oh no, honey. I didn't invite them. I didn't want the embarrassment that you're now suffering from."

"I didn't say that I was embarrassed, maybe for the stripper, but certainly not me. Besides, Ms. Alfreda is too busy waving money and telling the man to show her a little something, something. Actually, I'm a little scared for him."

"My point exactly, dear. We're having a good time. I'm sorry to hear that you are not.
Mother Rose sends you her love."

"May I speak to Mother Rose, please?"

"Sure, honey."

"Hey, my sweet girl, what's going on?"

"My granny and her friend crashed my bachelorette party."

"Really?"

"I didn't know my mother hadn't invited them to the tea."

"That is a shame to hear. I was wondering where they were. I enjoyed them this evening. Those ladies know how to live it up. Listen, you all are in the presidential suite, right?" Stephen's grandmother said.

"Yes, ma'am," Kenya answered, confused.

"Good, I'm coming over there because I'm sick of this stuffy crap. Give me some
Mandingo action any day, baby. I'll see you in a few, child." Mother Rose said, hanging up.

Kenya was so outdone, that she didn't know what to do. Never in her wildest dreams had she ever dreamt that she would spend her bachelorette night partying with her Granny. But as they say, if you can't beat them, join them. And just like that, Mother Rose was at the door with four of Stephen's great-aunts. Old school versus new school, Kenya hoped that the young man had the strength to take on all these women, and they didn't get kicked out of the hotel for getting too rowdy.

Chapter 13

That bachelorette party was one for the record books. Their nightly entertainment had to call in reinforcements. It turned out he had a twin that was a dancer as well. And if that wasn't enough, they decided to have a whining contest. Those island women showed those young girls a thing or two. Even the men got in on the action. Dawn Penn's, You Don't Love Me (No No No) brought the house down. These were some real dance hall queens. No twerking was necessary or needed with these sisters. One even yelled out, "Put your back into it, boy!"

Getting out of bed before noon was non-negotiable. By the time Birdie and Ms. Alfreda made it out of their room for lunch, Tylenol, Bengay, and Jesus had become their closest friends. They ordered room services for breakfast and agreed to meet in the lavish dining hall for lunch.

"Birdie, those strippers from last night, whew!" Alfreda exclaimed as she slowly took her seat.

"Honey, I know. I've never been so tired in all my life."

"Me either, Birdie. But girl, they got all my ones."

"You brought money with you?" Birdie asked her.

"You mean to tell me you didn't? Honey, I knew when they said bachelorette party to get my money ready. Chile that was the best five dollars I'd ever spent."

"Alfreda, you should have been ashamed caring on like that." Birdie told her.

"But I'm not. You should have gotten in on the action. I would've given you two of my dollars."

"Girl, you are a mess. Besides, I'm a happily married woman."

"Shoot, girl, I would've been happily married and had me some fun on the side. Last night I had fun for both of us." Alfreda told her.

"Yes, you did, and that's why we're both dragging today." Birdie said.

"I know somebody who is not that Pepper. This helfa had the nerve to call me first thing this morning while she was running on the treadmill. Honey, she was asking all kinds of questions. Chile, I just didn't have enough energy or the strength to answer. And after hanging up from her, her dad called. You know I didn't talk to him. I sent him straight to voicemail. She must have ratted me out. But I'll deal with him later."

"That sounds about right. She never could hold nothing. I guess she got that from you, too." Birdie said, laughing.

"I'm too tired to argue. Just know that I owe you one. What time is the rehearsal dinner?"

"I believe they said seven, but I don't know what they'll be serving. I'm not that worried because Walter has so many leftovers from last night, that he could have his own personal Caribbean night part two."

"He knows he ate up something. I'll tell you who will be sitting down and acting as if they got some sense tonight, me. I overdid it yesterday, and I'm really feeling it today."

"Do you think you need to have someone look at your hip?"

"The way some of those men in Stephen's family look, it'll definitely be one of them."

"Not all of them are doctors, silly woman."

"That's okay. I can play sick, too. Ouch. Oooh."

"Girl, you're crazy." Birdie said, laughing.

"You're laughing, but I'm serious. Especially the one with the whitish-gray locs. He had the smoothest Hershey brown skin. Lawd have mercy that man knows he's good looking!" She said, fanning herself with her napkin.

"I think that's Stephen's uncle."

"I wonder if he's single."

"I didn't see anyone with him at the dinner last night."

"Is he a doctor as well?"

"I believe so."

"Un-huh, that's what I'm talking about. I believe I need a check-up."

"I think he's an ear, nose, and throat doctor. Your problem is in the hip."

"Huh, what you say? I'm not hearing you so clearly these days?"

"Now I know you don't have right bright sense." Birdie said, laughing at Alfreda.

"Girl, they have some good-looking men in that family. Good gracious. And the ladies are super sweet, too." Alfreda said.

"I sure enjoyed myself with them last night. And you know, Mother Rose told me what she told Karen."

"What did she say?" Alfreda asked.

"She apologized for my not being invited. Had she known that I wasn't, she wouldn't have attended. She told me that's why they left."

"Girl, what!?"

"Yeah, she told me that was not how any family should act. She wanted me to know that their family wasn't that way. No matter who you are or where you come from, everyone is included. She took it as a personal insult that I was not there."

"Oh wow! That's right, Stephen's mother hosted that party. She left her own daughter's tea party and came to be with us. That was really nice of her."

"She told me before leaving that she told both her daughter and mine about how she felt about it too!"

"I wish I could have been a fly on the wall to see the look on Karen's face."

"Knowing her, she didn't care because she had all the people there, she wanted to impress."

"And that's a shame."

"But who I'm waiting on is Walter. He is the one." Birdie said, talking about her husband.

"That's true, Birdie, but what I don't get is why. Her husband is so down to earth, and if you didn't know who he was, you wouldn't know that his family had money."

"Yeah, but some people in his family act just like her, if not worse. Do you remember their big lavished wedding? We had to get her told then about what we were going to do, and what we weren't. If she thought that we were going to go broke so that she could have this fairytale wedding, she'd better think again. Kasey was in college, too. Girl, what she was asking for was outrageous. A ten thousand dollar dress, hmph. Honey, she had lost her mind for something that wasn't going to be worn but for hot a minute. I didn't care how mad at me she got. A crazy helfa ... talking about, we don't want to see her happy."

"Chile, that's just pitiful. That was a who's who type of affair. I never saw so many limos in my life and nobody had died."

"A spectacle is what it was. She got it back, though. His family gave her a run for her money in the beginning."

"I wouldn't have guessed in a million years that she'd marry somebody white," Alfreda said.

"All while she was in high school and some parts of college, all the guys she dated were black, but as fate would have it, they met in their junior year at the University of Denver, and they've been inseparable ever since."

"Girl, I remember when she brought Daniel home," Alfreda said, laughing at the memory.

"That boy could have been black as midnight, and Walter would have found fault with him. But Daniel won Walter over, and the rest for them is history. All I was concerned about was my baby not being mistreated because of the color of her skin. I wish that Daniel's parents were still alive to see their granddaughter's big day."

"Their deaths were such a tragedy. They never recovered their bodies, did they?"

"No, they were never found and to this day, no one knows what caused that boat to explode. Not one single surveyor family or crew. You know Daniel was supposed to be on that boat, but changed his mind at the last minute to go somewhere with Karen."

"Thank God, he did," Alfreda said.

"Yeah, I know. He always says Karen saved his life in more ways than he can count."

"They make a good-looking couple, and you can really tell they love each other. Most people just be pretending, like Patricia's granddaughter. Talking about Papa this and Papa that.

She's just full of crap."

"Girl, she knows she's not fooling anybody. That man is about fifty years her senior, if not more." Birdie said.

"She probably wakes up early in the morning just to put a mirror under his nose to see if he's still breathing," Alfreda said.

"As soon as he closes his eyes, that girl is going to catch hell. That family is going to fight her every which way but loose for that money."

"Baby, it takes Eloise to talk about how she has all these expensive shoes and handbags."

"Humph, she better get all she can while the getting is good now because she's gonna have to pawn or sell it later for the attorney fees," Alfreda said.

"Girl, you can't pawn shoes and purses." Birdie told her, laughing.

"Yes, you can too. I see it on TV all the time talking about selling your clothes and things."

"Now, who would want to buy somebody's worn goods?"

"Somebody who can't afford the whole price," Alfreda told her.

"Chile, what will they sell next, used draws, socks, and bras?" Birdie asked.

"I think that's where they draw the line, Birdie."

"But you know she has a lot to gain besides the money, his businesses, the houses, cars, and other properties." Birdie said.

"If you think his family is going to let her get her greedy paws on all of that stuff, I have a castle at Walt Disney World to sell to you."

"It's all about that will, Alfreda. If it's ironclad, there's nothing they can do to keep it from her."

"Other than having her come up missing, you right."

"That'll be about the only thing. But you know, like I do, if something like that should ever happen, you'd be the first one to start pointing fingers." Birdie told her, laughing.

"You know me so well. And it would be his family that I'd point at too."

"You got that right!"

"Birdie, I'm going to make my way back to the room. Chile, I think my medicine is kicking in." Alfreda said after looking at her phone.

"We sat here and talked so much and hadn't ordered a single thing. Let me place our orders to go, and I'll help you get to your room. You've scarred me one time too many already."

"I know, but honey, once these meds kick in, I don't trust me to spell 'I' right."

"Girl gone. You know you're a mess." Birdie said, laughing.

Chapter 14

Birdie helped Alfreda get to her room as promised. She told her that she would check on her a little later. She entered her room to see her husband move about as if he was in a hurry.

"Where are you off to, Walter?"

"Oh, I'm just stepping out for a minute. Is one of those mine?" He said, pointing to the carryout boxes she was holding.

"Oh shoot! I forgot to give Alfreda her food."

"If she left it, she didn't want it, so I'll eat it." He said, reaching for the plate.

"Oh no, you won't! I'm going to give this to her right now." She said.

Heading to the door, Walter blocks it. "What's the hurry?"

"Walter Abrams, you might as well move away from that door. You will not smooth talk me into giving you this food. Besides, I thought you were in a hurry."

"Nooo, I'm not in a hurry. But tell me something, what's in the box? He asked, standing there looking at her as if she was Little Red Riding Hood, and he was the big bad wolf with his tongue hanging out."

"If you must know, it is something healthy. It's just a salad."

"A salad!"

"Yes, eatem' up, a salad."

"Humph, you could've told me that in the first place. I thought you had something good in there."

"Salads are good."

"If you say so." He said, moving from the door.

"I do. But you wouldn't know from all the stuff you've been eating. A salad is what you need."

"I'll pass."

"Okay, but don't say nothing to me when you can't zip up your already let-out trousers next week."

"It ain't from that. I think them folks washing my clothes on the wrong cycle down there at that the cleaners. I have a right mind to go somewhere else, anyway."

"Oh yeah, and I guess you think they were the reason you popped two buttons on three different shirts, too."

"As a matter of fact, I do."

"Really Walter? You really believe the cleaners caused all of that and not your stomach?"

"Yes, it's them. I've been the same weight for the past twenty years."

"I guess you're also shrinking then, because the shorter you get, the wider you get." Birdie told him.

"Well, they do say you shrink as you get older," Walter told her.

"You know what . . . Bye Walter. I'm taking Freda her salad." She said, shaking her head at her husband as she left.

It took Alfreda a minute to open the door.

"Hey, Birdie," Alfreda spoke with the door cracked behind her.

"Here, honey, I brought you your salad." She said slowly and while looking at her strangely.

"Oh, thank you! I totally forgot about it."

"Un-huh, you changed clothes fast." She said, acknowledging Alfreda's bathrobe.

"Well yeah, I knew when I got back here that I was going to shower and get back into bed."

"Un-huh, well-gone head, and get your
rest. I'll check on you later." "Okay, talk to
you soon," Alfreda said, closing the door.

I'd be glad when she gets off that medication. That
stuff makes folks act all kinds of strange and thangs. Birdie
thought as she returned to her room.

Chapter 15

Birdie noticed that it had gotten late. Walter had already left to go to the rehearsal dinner. It was strange that she hadn't heard from Alfreda. They are early for almost everything. Birdie called Alfreda and became instantly worried when she didn't answer. "Now I know something is wrong. Lawd have mercy on my dear friend." Birdie rushed across the hall and banged on Alfreda's door. **"Alfreda, Alfreda!"** But there was no answer. She heard a door opening and was relieved to see a member of housekeeping leaving another room.

"Excuse me, ma'am, can you please help me?" Birdie asked. "My friend was not feeling well earlier today, and now she's not responding to my phone calls or answering her door. Please help me, please. **This is an emergency!**" She shouted, noticing the hesitation on the housekeeper's face. "If I didn't believe my friend was in trouble, I wouldn't ask. Please help me."

"Yes, ma'am, I'll help you." The housekeeper told her. "We wouldn't normally do this because you never know, but I see how worried you are about your friend."

"Thank you so much, sweetheart," Birdie told the housekeeper as the door was being opened. "If she's hurt, I don't know, I don't know what I'll..." was all Birdie could get out just before passing out.

Chapter 16

Birdie was awakened by her future grandson, and surrounded by many faces she had not committed to memory.

"Where am I? How did I get here?" Birdie asked as her head was still spinning. All she remembered seeing was a familiar robe, church socks, ashy knees, and white boxers with hearts on them.

"Oh my God, Birdie, are you alright!?" Alfreda asked as she looked on with the others. "She's going to be alright. Her breathing and heart rate have both returned to normal."

Stephen answered.

"Thank God." Alfreda said.

"Mom, what happened? The housekeeper said you were frantic and just passed out."

"I'm afraid this is all my fault," Alfreda confessed. "Had I answered the phone when she called, she wouldn't have fainted."

"You got that right!" Birdie said, rolling her eyes.

"It's nobody's fault," Walter chimed in. It's called minding the business that pays you."

"Walter, how dare you try to defend this...
this, whatever it is?" "Easy. It had nothing to
do with you." He said.

"Okay, okay. Ms. Birdie, you're getting too excited. It's causing more harm than good. May I suggest that you all discuss this later and focus on her remaining calm for the time being," Stephen told them.

"I don't think so! We're going to get to the bottom of this right now!" Birdie demanded.

"That's fine, but you'll be doing so from a hospital bed. That means you'll miss our wedding, and I know you wouldn't want to miss it but hey, the choice is yours." "Birdie, please don't make matters worse." Alfreda pleaded with her.

"Fine, but this isn't over." Birdie said, remembering why she didn't like doctors at times.

They always try to tell you what to do and be all in your business.

"I know, but please remain calm," Alfreda replied.

"Good. Everyone, let's let her rest tonight. I don't want you concerning yourself with anything or anyone tonight. We'll see you tomorrow." Stephen said, kissing her on the forehead.

He could tell by the frown on her face that she didn't like what he had said.

"Y'all go on ahead and have a wonderful dinner. I'm going to stay here with her," Alfreda told them.

"Are you sure?" Karen asked.

"Trust and believe me, she will not rest a single second if I don't," Alfreda said.

Chapter 17

The room had become awkwardly silent after everyone had left. "Can I get you something to eat, Birdie?" Alfreda asked.

"Drink is more like it, and make it strong." Birdie suggested.

"I have just the thing. I'll be right back." Alfreda said.

The awkwardness had returned once Alfreda left the room. The only thing that was left behind was an exchange of looks of guilt and shame. Birdie was sitting there in complete shock after what she had witnessed.

"Here we go," Alfreda said as she returned.

"Johnnie Walker! Now we're getting somewhere." Birdie said.

"Oh yeah, I brought it with me. I made a stop before going to the airport." Alfreda said.

"That ain't all you managed to bring with you," Birdie said, returning her gaze to the one sitting next to Alfreda.

"Yes, about that. I knew it was going to come as a shock to you, but I didn't know you'd take it like that."

"Helfa, I was worried about you! And when you didn't answer the phone or door, Lawd have mercy! Shoot, I didn't know what to think." She said, fanning herself because the whiskey had taken effect. "I thought you were dead or something. Lawd Jesus, you being with a man never even crossed my mind. But I'll tell you this, I knew it! **I knew it!** You can't fool these old bones, baby! I knew something was going on between you two." She exclaimed.

"Ms. Birdie, let me be the one to first apologize to you. I know we, Alfreda, and I

never meant to cause you any harm. I wanted you to know about us, but Walt told me to

wait."

"Well, Deacon Larry, I can't blame you, so I don't. The devil and his sister over there could have told me." Birdie said, rolling her eyes at her husband and friend. They knew she hated being the last one to know stuff.

"Honey, I apologize as well. The truth be told Birdie, had I not been stretching to see what Mr. Wilson had taken out of his house, you would have known everything that day, but the ladder leaned farther than I wanted it to, and down I went." Alfreda explained.

"I guess when the Lord says to mind your own business, He means it. Y'all better listen up." Walter declared.

"Walter, please, the Lord had nothing to do with Alfreda's falling, and you know it. It's

by His grace that fall didn't kill her." Birdie told him.

"All I know is, had she been minding her own business, she wouldn't have fallen."

Walter replied.

"And all I know is if you had cut them hedges down like I had asked you to, I wouldn't be missing anything." She told him. "Got me missing everything." Birdie mumbled under her breath.

"How you missed him, I don't know, Birdie. Who do you think called the ambulance?" He asked her.

"I promise you, I didn't see him. But anyway, Alfreda, what did he pull out of the house, girl?" She asked.

"Chile, nothing but some junk," Alfreda replied.

"Umph, I thought it was his son's things again. I don't know about anybody else, but I wouldn't stay with anybody that put my thangs out every other week. All he does is go from this one to that one. At his age, you'd think he'd be settled down somewhere."

"Well, the poor man is doing the best he can. When his wife gets tired of him, he goes to his girlfriend's house. When she gets tired of him, he goes to his parent's house. They treat him like a part-time parent. Everybody has visitation rights, but don't nobody want custody." Alfreda

told them.

"Girl, you need to stop," she said, laughing at Alfreda. "And I still can't believe you, Walter Abrams. You are a trip." Birdie told her husband.

"I wasn't going to say a word. For what, so that you could do what you're doing now,

interfere every chance you get, nope, I was not going to do it." Walter said as a matter of fact. "You got some nerve, Walter Abrams, I'll give you that, but you don't know what you think you do. Who do you think got them together?" Birdie asked.

"Huh!?" Everyone said in confusion.

"You must've really bumped your head when you passed out," Walter said, laughing.

"Alfreda and I were already friends for years before I started courting her," Larry said.

"Birdie, he's right. We were, you know that. Are you okay?" Alfreda asked, concerned.

"I'm fine. Thank you very much. Well, answer me this then, how did you all get together?" She asked them.

"Last year, after church service, there was a note I found on my windshield addressed to me. It asked me to come back to the sanctuary, but when I got there, only Alfreda was there collecting the hymnals." Larry told her.

"Then he asked me if I had written him a note, or knew who had," Alfreda replied. "Of course, I hadn't, but the writing looked familiar. By that time, the parking lot had emptied, and it was only us there. He helped me to store away the rest of the hymnals, invited me out for an early dinner, and the rest, as they say, is history." Alfreda explained.

"Who do you think wrote the note?" Birdie asked.

"Birdie, noooo. You did! Why?" Alfreda asked, shocked.

"Because y'all were taking too long. I've been telling you about Deacon Larry for years, Alfreda. I had to get the ball rolling somehow, so I sent the note. Ernestine Billups had her good eye on him, plus Margaret Ann Mitchell had already wiggled her way in the picture, but by the looks of things, that didn't last too long." Birdie said.

"Oh my God, I can't believe you did that, Birdie," Alfreda said, flushed.

"Birdie, what are you talking about? You don't have all your facts straight. Ernestine

Billups is seeing Deacon Whatley." Walter told her.

"She's what!?" Both she and Alfreda said.

"Um, um, um. What a pair, what a pair?" Birdie commented.

"See, that right there is why I don't tell you anything. Birdie, you always got something to say about people."

"I hadn't said a word, Walter. But you must admit, they are quite a pair." Birdie said, laughing to herself.

"Stay out of them folks' business, Birdie," Walter demanded.

"Why? Just because she's six foot seven, and he's five foot two, the whole world can see that as being interesting. I don't have a single thing to do with that." Birdie said.

"You know his last wife was tall, too. He might have a thing for tall women." Alfreda

said.

"Un-huh, one of those Neapolitan complexes."

"Naw Birdie, that's Napoleon. Neapolitan is the ice cream." Alfreda said.

"Oh yeah. I used to buy that ice cream all the time. I believe the strawberry was my favorite out of the three." Birdie replied.

Walter looked at his wife and her friend in disbelief. "Are you sure you want to be in this circle of crazy?" He asked Larry, who was laughing at the two ladies. Their conversation had gone from people with complexes to who had the best ice cream brand.

"Yes, I'm very sure," Larry replied. "I haven't been this happy in a long time." "You'll be in my deepest of prayers, my brother," Walter told him.

"Do you all remember that Sunday when they announced the passing of Sister Whatley?" Larry asked them.

"I sure do. I thought somebody was going to have to carry me out of there."

Alfreda said. "Birdie, you remember that Sunday?"

"Oh yeah, I will never forget that as long as I live." She told them. "I thank God that man was not in service that day, because he'd never speak to me again. Sister Jones had walked up there to that podium all prim and proper and said, "Please keep the Whatley family in your prayers as Sister Whatley has lost her battle to prostate cancer." And out of nowhere, in a quiet church, Reverend Sherman croaks out, "**She what!**" Birdie said, imitating the Reverend Sherman.

"Ooh chile, the way the congregation laughed that day. Sister Jones had literally turned purple because she could not figure out why everyone was laughing." Alfreda said.

"The first lady helped her out by making the correction of colon, not prostate," Birdie said, laughing.

"But that didn't help matters when Reverend Sherman said, "Well, thank God for that, because if she had a prostate, we all needed answers. But we will keep the Whatley family in our prayers." Alfreda said, fighting back the tears from laughing so hard.

"Man, don't you let them tie you into their mess. Are you sure that you want to live like this?" Walter asked, laughing, remembering the events.

"What are you over there griping about now, Walter?" Birdie asked him.

"Nothing. I was just asking Larry if he was sure about something."

"Sure about what?" Birdie asked.

"Something I was going to tell you about before all the excitement took place," Alfreda said.

"I asked Alfreda to marry me, Ms. Birdie. And she said yes." He said proudly.

"Hallelujah!" Birdie shouted, waving her hands in the air. "We are going to have us a church wedding."

"Whooooa, Birdie...we haven't discussed this with our families yet. But I can tell you this right now. It's going to be something very simple and small. We don't have a single soul to impress."

"Chile, the way things are going today, these couples are spending thousands of dollars just to be married for two minutes." Birdie said.

"And to be honest, I was thinking the same thing. We don't need anyone there but family and close friends." Larry said.

Before, Birdie could add two more of her cents, Walter chimed in, "Since the cat is out of the bag, I guess we can celebrate."

"Not so fast, Walter. So you knew about this too, and didn't tell me? Just when you think you know a person. Just a shame, just a shame."

"Naturally, I told Walter. He was with me when I picked out the ring." Larry said.

"It's not a shame, Birdie. I just know how to keep things to myself."

"See, that's my problem with you, Walter. You shouldn't have kept anything that good to yourself."

"Birdie, you would've told Alfreda everything as sure as my name is Walter
James Abrams."

"That's beside the point. You should've told me, anyway. I wouldn't have been worried, and ended up on that questionable cleaned floor." Thinking back on seeing Larry in his boxers, she continued, "I'd rather not discuss this anymore. See, I too know how to keep a secret."

"Miracles do exist," Walter replied.

"On that note, we'll just say goodnight. I'm going to treat my fiancé to a candlelight dinner for two." Larry said as he and Alfreda walked to the door. "Well, goodnight," Birdie said, wishing she could ask Alfreda more questions, like why was Deacon Larry in his boxers and church socks. But it'll have to wait until tomorrow, she guessed. "We'll see y'all tomorrow." Birdie said, walking to the door.

"What a blessing! Walter, our good friends have gotten together." Birdie said, beaming as she locked the door. "And you know Deacon Larry has been liking her for years."

"I really wouldn't have known."

"You wouldn't have known Walter because you don't pay attention to things like I do."

"You mean I don't put myself in other folk's business the way you do."

"Say what you will, but I was spot on about this one. And if you weren't so busy reading that room service menu, you'd admit that I was right."

"Un-huh, are you getting anything to eat?" Walter asked, knowing full well that he wasn't about to admit a thing. To do so, he'd never hear the end of it. Let her tell it, she's right about everything.

Chapter 18

The day had finally come for Kenya and Stephen to become one, and the pair couldn't be any happier. Even with the scare of seeing her grandmother laid out on the floor last night, the way her husband to be took charge, let her know that if there were any lingering doubts, they no longer existed. She remembered how she and Stephen were on their way to check on her grandparents when they saw Alfreda, a man in his boxers, and the housekeeper standing over her grandmother. She and Stephen took off running toward them. Once Stephen was able to revive her grandmother, he picked her up and carried her to her room.

That was the scariest thing she'd ever encountered. As a nurse, she'd seen many things, but when it's your family or someone you love, things become different. But Stephen stepped right in, and from that moment, she knew he would do whatever it took to take care of her and their family. That moment caused her to fall in love with him all over again.

Kenya's thoughts were interrupted when her dad spoke. "Alright Princess, they are playing our song." Her father said, getting ready to walk her down the aisle. "You look so beautiful, sweetheart," He said, trying to fight back his tears. "I have to tell you this. I'm so proud of the woman you've become. And it is an honor to be your dad. You were raised in a house truly built on love, and I pray that God blesses you and Stephen with the same and more."

"Oh my God, Daddy." She says, hugging him tightly, "You're going to make me mess up my makeup." She told him, trying not to cry. But Kenya couldn't help it. Her heart was full and overflowed with gratefulness.

***

"Birdie, that wedding was absolutely beautiful. All white everything. Girl, that's what I call a classy affair." Alfreda said as she and Birdie sat at the table waiting for Walter and Larry to return with their refreshments.

"It really was, and girl, her dress." Birdie said.

"Oh my, honey, wasn't that dress beautiful?"

"Chile, that dress was so sharp, it could've walked down the aisle by itself. It was too sharp!"

"Everybody and everything was beautiful. I loved their wedding theme too: ivory, crystal, and pearl. It was just simply beautiful." Alfreda said.

"Now you know they spent a lot of money," Birdie said, looking around.

Alfreda, doing the same, whispered, "Girl, I'm not surprised or shocked. Ain't nothing in this room but what-..."

"Money." Birdie added.

"You better say that again. But I ain't mad at them. You can't take it with you and that's for sure. This week don't owe me nothing, honey. It blessed me to be amongst them. Maybe some of them dollars can rub off on me." Alfreda said.

"For what? So that you can go and rub them on somebody else."

"Mind your business, they don't owe me nothing either," Alfreda said, laughing.

"I know they don't, especially when you also had a half-naked man in your room. Oh, you know I was going to get back to the nitty-gritty." Birdie said, looking around.

"Birdie, you got this all wrong," Alfreda said, ashamed.

"Honey, I know what I saw with my own two eyes."

"Birdie, as long as we'd been friends, I've never lied to you. It is true, I was dishonest about Larry, but I'm telling you, you got this all wrong." Alfreda said sincerely.

"What do you mean?" Birdie asked.

"How Larry ended up in his boxer shorts was all my fault," Alfreda explained.

"Do tell." Birdie said, grinning.

"No, not like that. We were sitting there drinking red wine when he proposed. Girl, that ring came out, and that wine went everywhere. Oh God, I'm still embarrassed. Birdie, I threw that wine all over Larry."

"Oh, no!" Birdie said, covering her mouth.

"Chile, he was wearing a cream-colored sweater and khaki pants. I tried everything I could to get those stains out of his clothes. That's what we were doing when you called." "Oh, my goodness. When I saw you in your robe and him in his shorts, well, I thought, as children can say, y'all was getting y'all freak on." "Really, Birdie?" Alfreda asked.

"Well, what else could I have thought? You didn't answer the phone or come to the door.

Shoot, honey, I remember them days like they were yesterday, young and frisky."

"Birdie, no. And anyway, that is not a robe that I wear, it's my caftan. You know how much I love wearing those things." Alfreda explained.

"Ooops." Birdie said, sheepishly smiling and covering her mouth.

"Ooops indeed," Alfreda said.

"I'll tell you one thing, it may have taken you and Larry forever to get together, but I am so glad y'all finally did. God knew you needed him. You remember that date you almost went on that would've required an attorney and some bail money?" Birdie asked, laughing.

"Honey, don't even talk about it." Alfreda said.

"Girl, if you could have only seen your face that day, that man called you from jail. Honey, I hollered." Birdie told her. "Girl, you hung the phone up faster than they could say book him. Who goes to jail for unpaid parking tickets, anyway?" She asked. "After that happened, you left that Sexy Single Seniors online group alone. The only thing you could've been for him was his pen pal. There's no telling how many men online was there trying to get a woman's social security check." Birdie said.

"I knew not mine, because I had no intentions of sharing. Girl, that was so many moons ago. Why bring it up now?" Alfreda asked her, laughing. "So that you'll appreciate the blessing you have now."

"Listen, I'm one divorce down and way too many bad relationships not to."

As the men returned, placing their drinks down, Birdie said, "Let's toast, here's to us, the good, the bad, and the-"

"Nosey," Walter said, interrupting Birdie's toast.

"Here's to us." They said, laughing.

"Now that y'all are back, tell us more about Ernestine Billups and Deacon Whatley?" Birdie asked.

"My name is Wes and I'm not in that mess," Walter said.

"And my name is Lar, and I wasn't there," Larry said.

"You're catching on, brother, you're catching on," Walter said, laughing. "And that's why some things should stay just between us." Walter told him.

"That's okay, y'all don't have to say a word, and we'll get our information because the streets are always talking." Birdie told them.

"I know that's right! They don't call them the street committee for nothing. Our information is only one coffee and cake invite away." Alfreda added.

"Lord, give us strength," Walter said, shaking his head as he thought about the parade of people that were about to descend upon his home. You can try to keep the best of secrets, but like a good hound dog, the snoop will always sniff them out. "Just the person I've been wanting to see." He said, as Karen was walked up to their table.

"Hello everyone." Karen said, greeting them.

"Karen." Birdie replied, knowing all hell was about to break loose.

"Baby girl, let me talk to you for a second. No, Birdie, you stay." He stated when he noticed her getting ready to stand. "Karen and I have some things to discuss."

"Lawd, be with her." Alfreda said, as she watched Walter and Karen walk away.

"Honey, the way she has treated us over the years, she has this conversation coming. No time for regrets and tears now. Honor thy mother and father. That's what the Word says." Birdie said.

"Girl, you're right, but the tongue lashing he's about to unleash on her is going to take God to intervene." Alfreda said, laughing.

"I'm sure this is going to hurt him more than it'll ever hurt her. He thinks the world of our daughter. But this is long overdue, and I'm finally glad everything I've known for years is out in the open."

"Secrets can hurt and destroy a family if things aren't resolved." Larry said.

"Hopefully, this will lead to healing." Alfreda said.

"Let's hope so." Birdie replied as they all watched.

Chapter 19

"Have a seat my daughter." Walter said, pulling out a chair for Karen at an empty table.

"Uh-oh, this must be something serious. You've never called me daughter unless I was in some sort of trouble." She replied.

"Trouble is one thing, but this is troubling. It is to my understanding that your mother was intentionally uninvited to your tea the other night." He said.

"Daddy, she wouldn't be comfortable around those kind of people."

"What kind of people wouldn't she be comfortable being around that you yourself can find comfort in?" He asked her.

"But I-," Karen tried to find the words to explain, but there were none.

"Let me make something clear to you, and I mean this from the bottom of my heart. Your mother and I may not have the education or the occupation that we blessed you with, but there is not a circles that she or myself can't walk or travel. No, we haven't traveled the world or experienced many things as you have, but that does not make us lesser than anyone else. How dare you treat the woman that gave you everything she could to be where you are today with such disrespect?" He asked her. "You should be ashamed of yourself. We didn't raise you, Karen, to look down on people for what they did not have. I will not tolerate this level of disrespect for your mother. You can continue to treat me however you wish, but as for my wife, your mother, you will not. I have never been so disappointed in you as I am now. You have hurt me deeply, Karen, but you have hurt your mother more. You may want to take a hard look at yourself in the mirror, baby. The person you've become is not the loving daughter that I cherish.

You have allowed money and influence to turn you into someone I don't know. She is cruel and hateful. This is not the daughter that I raised and love. When you find her, you let me know." He said, standing to leave.

"Oh daddy, I'm so sorry. Please don't go." Karen said, sobbing in Walter's arms. To hear her father say that she was cruel and hateful tore Karen's heart into pieces. She never saw herself in this way. It was true that she had become embarrassed by her parents, but that was her view. No one else saw them in this way. She was wrong, and she knew it. There was nothing left for her to do but beg her parents for forgiveness.

When Birdie saw Karen crying, she knew Walter had lit into her. But she was her baby, no matter what. Birdie did what any loving parent would do, held her daughter as she cried and forgave her. It was as if she were a small child, helpless. She took Karen to the bathroom to help clean her up. While there, Karen apologized for everything and promised to change. Birdie loved her daughter and had already forgiven her, but if she never invites her to one of those uppity affairs, she wouldn't be disappointed. She liked to be around down-to-earth people, her kind of people.

The End . . . Probably Not!

Thank you for reading Peepers2!
Coming in 2023...
A new drama series is headed your way!
Turn the page for your sneak peek!

A Thin line Between Lust and Love
. . . Secret Affairs
    A Novel Written by
    Author D. D. Miles

Chapter 1
BENJAMIN

I have so much on my mind right now. The last place I needed to be was here. Mentally, my mind was across town, but physically, my body is sitting on the first pew of St. Peter's Baptist Church next to my mother, the First Lady. She was glad that I could attend service today, and would have been happier, had my brother or I followed in the footsteps of our father, the Pastor. But my brother and I knew all too well that many were called and only a few were chosen, and we were neither the chosen nor the called.

Our parents naturally assumed that we would have joined the ministry, because that's what Pop did, and his father before him. Years ago, he approached us about going to seminary school, but we told our parents that we wanted a different career path. This, however, didn't go over too well in the beginning. Pop's argument was one of us should follow in his footsteps, regardless.

"Who's going to take over as pastor after I'm gone, if neither one of my own sons won't, or just flat out refuse to? That church has been in our family for over sixty years. This is the very same church that helped raise your ungrateful behinds, and you two won't even give it a second thought to carry on your father's family tradition. That's just shameful!" Pop said, fussing at us. I later found out this was not so much as us not wanting to become ministers that upset Pop, as it was us not wanting to be just like him.

At that time, I just knew he was going to kick us out of his house and disown us, but he didn't. As time went on, thankfully, Pop stopped riding our backs and finally accepted our decisions for what they were. Because I for one, was not about to step into anybody's pulpit, talking about what thus saith the Lord when I lived how I wanted and did as I pleased. No sir, right or wrong, I had enough to give in account for, and leading people to hell on the account of my own actions was not going to be on that list.

After the choir finished singing their last selection, Pop walked up to the podium to introduce his message. He told us to turn our Bibles to 2 Corinthians 5:17. As Pop spoke, his voice faded as my mind drifted back to my own life's dilemma. The problem is that I'm seeing a woman and my feelings for her have become very strong, but there's someone else too. I know I have to cut the other woman out of my life for good, but how?

The how part was finally coming, that was, until he startled me back into reality. Pop was standing in front of me, **"Are you a new man, son?!"** He shouted, with his mic in one hand, and pointing his index finger at me with the other.

Stunned, all I could do at first was nod my head up and down. "Yes sir. I am a new man,"

I finally replied.

Indeed, I was a new man, but for another reason. This one-woman had changed my entire outlook on life as I knew it.

"Are you a new man in Christ, church? If so, let the church say amen." Pop said as he closed out his sermon. There were amens, hallelujahs, and preach preachers being shouted all over the sanctuary. I was glad Pop was wrapping service up, because I was ready to feed my face.

I took my parents to one of our favorite family barbeque spots. Like any other place on

Sunday afternoon, it was jam-packed, but we didn't have to wait long.

"Thank you, son, for taking us to dinner, but you know I'd rather cook." Ma said as we were being seated.

That's my momma always taking care of us. She was the most thoughtful person I knew.

"That's okay Ma. I enjoy spending time with you and Pop."

"What did you get out of my sermon today, son?" He asked, looking me square in the eyes after setting aside his menu.

"A lot. You really had them riled up today."

"Please, that was the Lord. I'm merely His messenger." He said, correcting me.

"I'm going to download today's service and review it when I get a chance."

"Un-huh, just what I thought. You weren't paying any attention today."

"Greg, you leave my baby alone. He just got home from a business trip. It's a wonder that he made it to church at all."

"Ah, Gloria, I just wanted to know if he received anything out of it," he said, getting ready to gripe about her being too overprotective.

I had to jump in before this became World War III. My momma always took up for us. I guess she thought Pop was always riding us, and it wasn't true. He just wanted us to be the men he raised us to be, by putting God first and allowing the rest to follow.

"Pop, I promise to rewatch the sermon from today, and all the others I missed from a couple of weeks ago."

"That's good son, but let me ask you something, that is, if mother hen over here don't mind." He said, looking at Ma, who then rolls her eyes at him. He winked at her, trying to make her blush, and it worked. Despite him being who he was, his only weakness was her, and he couldn't stand her being mad at him. "Who's this young lady that had your thoughts today?" Pop had caught me off guard with his question. Ma had even put her fork down and stopped chewing her salad just to hear my response. Because they knew I rarely brought or mentioned any women to them. Not that they would like the type of women I sometimes kept company with now and then.

I stopped bringing my playmates around because Ma would go into instant wedding planner mode.

"What do you mean, Pop?" I said, trying to play him off the question.

"What I mean is, who had your attention today other than thus saith the Lord?"

"Ah Pop, it's not even like that. I mean, I was thinking of someone, but you know what I'm saying." I said, hoping he would just let me off the hook, but fat chance.

"Yeah son, I know. So who is she?"

I sighed. "Her name is Tamara Reed."

"Her name is pretty. When will you bring her to church and let us meet her?" Ma asked.

"Soon, I promise."

"I don't know about you, Gloria, but I, for one, will be glad when he does. ' Cause I get so tired of people dragging their single daughters up to us after church, and introducing them as if we don't already know them. Then to top it off, asking us where are you and your brother, like we arrange marriages or something."

"I'm sorry, Pop, but you and Ma were blessed to have two handsome, successful sons. It comes with the territory," I said, popping my collar. "We can't help it if the ladies love us," I said, laughing.

"Y'all can't help it alright. I'll tell you what, if you don't bring this new girl to church soon, I will raffle off your home phone number for the youth's scholarship fund. I know that will bring in a hefty dollar," he said, laughing. "Yeah buddy. We would make fundraising history with that one. Over a million dollars within the first hour. Folks would take out payday loans and second mortgages just to get those seven digits. We'd probably have enough money to send these kids to college twice. Watch and see."

"No need, Pop, she'll be there. I have finally found the one. Don't be shocked by the admission, but it's so true." I told them, laughing at the shock on both of their faces.

"Really Benji," Ma asked, smiling. I could see the wheels in her pretty head-turning. I bet she had a catering company on speed dial.

"Yes ma'am. She's very special, and I can't wait for both of you to meet her. I know I have a good thing, and I'm planning to do all I can to make Tamara happy." I told my parents all about her and promised to bring Tamara to church next Sunday.

After sharing a meal with my parents, I returned home and continued to ponder my situation. The task before me wasn't hard, but the outcome could be dramatizing. I knew Stacy could be a drama queen, but she was the past. This had to be done in order to completely embrace Tamara, my future. My future possessed everything I ever wanted and needed.

At first, when I met Tamara, I wanted to take things really slow with her. "Take your time, no need to rush," is what I kept telling myself, but once I fell in love with her, I didn't need or want anyone else. In her, I had everything. She's smart and beautiful. I fell in love with her sexy almond shape, light brown eyes first and then her devilish dimples second. There are no words that I could possibly form to express how I was feeling when I first meet her. Tamara's skin tone reminded me of honey, the sweetest shade of brown with golden undertones, and whether or not she knew it, her lips begged me to taste them. She had a body so bangin, that she'd make an hourglass jealous. A perfect ten with curves galore with legs that went on for days. I knew once I got a chance to be with her, I was going to make her mine forever. She was the only woman for me, but before I can be hers exclusively, I have to end my relationship with Stacy.

It's not going to be easy. I've tried to call it off with her once before. That didn't last too

long, because she knew what I liked. Stacy had developed feelings for me. Even though we agreed on what type of relationship we were going to have, she had a change of plans. Just the thought of going through this again with her was causing me to have a headache, but I loved Tamara too much, not to. I would do whatever it took to secure our future. I picked up the phone and dialed Stacy's number. When she answered, I took a deep breath, and then spoke.

"Stacy, it's me. I need to see you. It's important. Can I come by?"

"You know my door is always open to you. Just come on over. Besides, I was just thinking about you. It's such a pretty day. Maybe we can keep it indoors, or we can do something like a picnic outdoors. When you get here, I will let you decide." She said.

"I won't be there long, I'll see you in twenty minutes. Bye," I said before hanging up.

A part of me wished I didn't have to do this face to face. She didn't have the slightest idea of what was about to happen. I didn't make it a habit to hurt people, but to tell her it was over between us over the phone was not good enough. She had to see that I was serious.

When I arrived, Stacy greeted me at the front door wearing a see-thru teddy. *"I made the decision to keep it inside,"* she told me, then wrapped her arms around my neck and kissed me passionately. I really didn't want to go there with her, this time especially, but seeing her like this just drove me crazy. The physical was never a problem, it was the basis of our so-called, "special friendship." And with us, one thing always led to another.

Just dumb. . . I thought to myself as I lay there with my hands covering my face, asking myself why I had to go and do this. Feeling guilty for what I just allowed to happen, I sat up to look around the floor for my clothes. I had to finish what I originally came there to do, no matter how uncomfortable it was going to be. I allowed myself to be sidetracked once, but never again.

This had to come to an end, now. She lifted her head and looked over at me.

"Where are you going?" She asked with a look of confusion on her face.

"I'll be right back."

I got out of her bed, grabbed all my belongings, and went into the bathroom. I felt so horrible, talk about dumb decisions. It was never my intent to sleep with her, but I can't deny it. Sex with Stacy was amazing. Still, I had to be a man about my business. When I returned, she was sitting on the edge of her bed wearing a short floral chemise robe and a smile. With my head held down, I reentered her bedroom. Under my breath, I apologized. I only took a few steps before Stacy met me midway. I looked into her eyes, held her hands, and I told her as calmly as I could, "I can't see you anymore."

Like a storm of fury, Stacy snapped as she snatched her hands away from me.

"How in the hell you just gon come up in here, make love to me like that, then just tell me that you can't see me anymore?!" She yelled.

"Stacy, I'm sorry. I've been seeing someone else, and I didn't mean for any of this to happen. I have somebody now, and you have to understand. It's not as if you don't have somebody too. Besides, aren't you tired of sneaking around on ol' boy?"

"Oh, baby, don't act as if you care now. Especially when you've been sleeping with his fiancée for months."

"His what?! Stacy look," I said with irritation. "I will not argue with you. We just need to move on with our lives, and let it be at that." I was not about to play this game of going back and forth.

"Move on, Benjamin? How am I suppose to do that? He doesn't make me feel the way you do. You know how to touch me, how to hold me, kiss me. I rarely even sleep with him, just because he's not you. Benjamin, how can you really expect me to move on without you?" She

said, full of dramatic movements and gestures, and one crocodile tear. And the Oscar goes to...

Now she's trying to toy with my ego, saying anything for me to buy into her hopes of keeping what we had together. I had to suppress my laughter because she was a drama queen to

the fullest.

"Then why are you marrying him? That's kind of selfish, don't you think? I mean, you are sleeping with him, wishing it were me, right? Stacy, I'm sorry, but I've got to go."

"Ben, you know you and I are good for each other. Why end this, just because you've met someone?"

"You are in a serious relationship with someone else, remember, and besides, I no longer want to be a part of this one," I told her.

"I don't want this to be goodbye for us."

"Stacy, I'm sorry, but we can't see each other anymore," I said once more.

"Well, I don't want to hear that!" She yelled. "What . . . what if I broke up with him, and just started seeing you, then could we be together?"

"Stacy, I'm seeing someone, just in case you didn't hear me the first two times."

"I'll give him back his ring, and call off the wedding," she said, obviously ignoring me.

"Why would you do that? You obviously loved him enough to accept his proposal."

"Because he's not you!" She shouted.

"Stacy, why are you making this so hard?" I yelled back. I was tired of her yelling at me.

"How hard do you think this is for me? Huh? Don't you get it? I've fallen in love with you!"

"Once again, I'm sorry, Stacy. I hope one day that you'll be able to forgive me," I said, turning to leave.

"Wait, before you go, I have one question. Who is she?"

"Excuse me?"

"Who is this person that you are leaving me for?!" She shouted.

"Goodbye Stacy," I said, walking out of her bedroom, heading for the front door.

"Fine! Forget you! Get out of my house, and don't you ever say another word to me, as long as you live! I hate you, Benjamin. I hate you!"

I left Stacy screaming at me as I walked out of her life. The first time should have been the last time, but she kept me coming back for more. Sex with her was very good. She knew exactly how to get me off without me saying one word.

We had an understanding from the beginning. We were just good friends with benefits, nothing more, and nothing less. I didn't get into her personal life, and she didn't get into mine.

But when I wanted to see her, I wanted to see her. That's it, no excuses.

Stacy played herself. She allowed herself to become caught up. I just sat back and reaped the benefits. Hell, she was the one putting it out there. What was I supposed to say, "No, thank you?"

She was the last dilemma of my past. Now that I have gladly turned over a new leaf in my life, I was no longer looking to divide and conquer new enticing territories. I knew where my heart was, and it was with Tamara, the love of my life.

www.ingramcontent.com/pod-product-compliance
Lightning Source LLC
Chambersburg PA
CBHW030508130626
46549CB00007B/2888